## Creative Team

**Co-founders & Directors**
Debbie and Phil Waldrep

**Creative Director**
Thomas Schwindling

**Content Editor**
Mackenzie Borden

**Cover Design**
Hannah Busing

**Typesetting**
Angela Davidson

COURAGE TO STAND

Copyright © 2022
By Debbie and Phil Waldrep

Published in Decatur, Alabama by Women of Joy. Women of Joy is a registered trademark of Phil Waldrep Ministries.

ISBN 978-1-7323687-4-3

*Unless otherwise indicated, all Scripture quotations are from The ESV® Bible (The Holy Bible, English Standard Version®), copyright © 2001 by Crossway, a publishing ministry of Good News Publishers. Used by permission. All rights reserved.*

*Printed in The United States of America*

**@womenofjoy**

**womenofjoy.org**
**1.800.374.1550**

## This Study Belongs To

_____

_____

## Start Date

_____ / _____ / _____

# COURAGE TO STAND

## AN EIGHT WEEK BIBLE STUDY ON ESTHER

**DEBBIE & PHIL WALDREP**

FOUNDERS AND HOSTS OF WOMEN OF JOY

# Debbie & Phil Waldrep

---

Courage is a virtue rarely applauded until someone practices it and our lives are made better for it.

At our Women of Joy events, we seek to inspire women to courageously face the challenges of life, encourage them to stand for what is right, and to inform them with biblical principles that make courage possible.

The "Courage to Stand" Bible study takes every woman deeper into how and why they should stand for what is right. Based on the Book of Esther, this study explores the fear and uncertainty, along with the positive effects of a courageous, godly woman who stands for her family, her community, and, most of all, herself.

With an open Bible and a pen, ask our Lord to speak to you from His Word. Listen as the Holy Spirit uses the life of Esther to guide you in the problems and situations of your life.

As a result, we are praying that you will realize that our Heavenly Father has placed you where you are to be His representative. "Who knows whether you have not come to the kingdom for such a time as this?" (Es. 4:14)

*Debbie + Phil*

Debbie and Phil Waldrep
Co-founders & Directors
Women of Joy

# Table of Contents

---

# Courage to Stand

"Wait for the Lord; be strong, and let your heart take courage; wait for the Lord!"

Psalm 27: 14

---

On December 1, 1955, a young woman stood on a street corner in Montgomery, Alabama waiting for a city bus to arrive. Moments later, she boarded the bus and took her seat in the "colored" session. When a white man stepped onto the bus and the "white" section was full, the bus driver told her to move to the back and give her seat to the white man.

Rosa Parks, the young lady sitting in the seat, refused. She courageously sat in her seat. The police were called, and they arrested her.

Although other African Americans refused to give up their seats before that day and they too were arrested, the arrest of Rosa Parks was the catalyst for launching the civil rights movement that ended segregation.

Rosa Parks, a committed Christian, believed segregation was wrong and decided to do something about it. It took courage to act. Later in life, she was recognized for her action, including being the first woman to lie in honor in the Rotunda of the United States Capitol.

The courage Mrs. Parks demonstrated didn't come easy. As a result of her actions, her employer fired her. She received death threats and was often mistreated. She never regretted what she did.

We often applaud courage after the fact, rarely before. We admire it and appreciate it, especially when the courage of another person helps us.

It is easier to describe courage than it is to define it.

Courage is the ability to face an obstacle and refusing to back down. It is the ability to endure pain or danger for the greater good.

Courage is the opposite of cowardice. Instead of running in fear, courage walks forward in faith.

Courage overcomes fear because something more important than personal discomfort must be done.

Courageous people are brave. They become our heroes. We admire them and applaud them. Yet, living courageously is hard.

C.S. Lewis may have given us the best definition of courage when he wrote, "Courage is not simply one of the virtues but the form of every virtue at its testing point."

**1** What Bible character do you think best demonstrated courage? Why? How do their actions encourage you?

_____

_____

_____

_____

_____

_____

_____

_____

_____

_____

_____

_____

_____

_____

The Bible is filled with people who faced foes greater than themselves and succeeded in what God called them to do.

Noah courageously built an ark when people were mocking him.

Moses demonstrated courage when he risked his life to confront Pharaoh and lead the Israelites out of Egyptian bondage.

David killed Goliath when all other soldiers, including King Saul, lacked the courage to fight in the name of the Lord.

Courage empowered Shadrach, Meshach, and Abednego to enter Nebuchadnezzar's fiery furnace and it helped Daniel resist the orders to pray to the king instead of God, knowing he would be thrown into the lion's den as a result.

And courage enabled Paul to fearlessly face execution because he knew what awaited him in heaven.

These stories are well known to most of us. We heard them in Bible stories as children and in sermons as adults. All of these Bible characters demonstrated the power of faith expressed in courage when following our Lord's commands.

**2** One Old Testament personality that needed courage was Joshua, the appointed leader of the Israelites after Moses. Leading a nation into a new land, fighting battles, and organizing the conquered lands was not easy.

Read Joshua 1. Three times God told Joshua to be of "good courage."

Looking at the list below, circle the things that characterize "good" courage.

Acting to impress people      Following God's will

Helping Others      Acting foolishly

Trying to prove a point      Obeying Scripture

Most of the stories of courageous acts we think about being in the Bible involve men, but the Bible records the courage of numerous women as well. Some are well-known and often are mentioned in church. Their stories fill many verses in the Bible. Others are lesser-known, but their stories fulfilled God's plan and they deserve consideration too.

In this study, we will explore the life of a courageous woman, Esther, and a courageous man, Mordecai. Their courage – individually and collectively – saved the lives of thousands of Jews.

Their story will encourage you. Seeing their struggles, the problems they faced, and, most of all, their courage, will inspire you to face the challenges you have.

**3** What is one area where you need the Lord to give you courage? Use these lines to write a prayer, asking God to give you the courage to act with "good" courage.

_____

_____

_____

_____

_____

_____

Week One

# Courage to Stand :
## COURAGE TO SAY NO

"But Queen Vashti refused to come at the king's command delivered by the eunuchs."

Esther 1:12a

---

In 2008, ABC started broadcasting a new television show called "What Would You Do?" The show used actors to create a situation where a person was being harassed or needed some help, such as a parent verbally abusing a child or an employee mistreating a customer. The actions always occurred in front of bystanders who were unaware of the show's filming. The purpose was to see if the bystanders would intervene and, if so, how.

After a scene played out, the host would appear and talk to the bystanders. He asked why they did or did not react the way they did. Interestingly, many of the people said they "had to do something" while others said, "they didn't want to get involved."

**1**   **Have you ever intervened to protect or help someone? Has someone intervened for you? Write about your experiences here.**

Whether you intervened or someone intervened for you, it took courage. Courage prompts you to do right when quitting would be more comfortable.

In the Old Testament, there is a story of a very courageous woman named Esther who intervened to save the lives of many Jews. The book is named after her, making it only one of two books in the Bible named after a woman (the other one is Ruth).

Interestingly, the book of Esther doesn't mention God or any spiritual activity like prayer or praising God. The New Testament never refers to the book of Esther. This doesn't mean that the book isn't divinely inspired, but it demonstrates how God is often working behind the scene to keep his promises.

The story of Esther begins in the third year of the reign of Ahasuerus. Ahasuerus wasn't the name of a person, it was the title for the Persian ruler like Pharaoh was for Egypt and Caesar was for Rome. Historians identify him as Xerxes, the king who reigned over Persia from 486-465 B.C. He was the grandson of Cyrus the Great.

When Xerxes became king at 32 years old, his empire stretched from India to Ethiopia, covering 127 provinces. Governors called satrapies helped him rule over his vast kingdom. Having several homes as kings usually do, Xerxes ruled from one of his four capitals based on the season. The story of Esther that we will be studying takes place at Susa, the king's winter palace.

 **Powerful people, especially those who have the power to affect our lives, are intimidating. Read I Samuel 17 about David killing Goliath. What caused the Israelites to fear? What gave David courage? Using I Samuel 17:45, complete this verse:**

**"Then David said to the Philistine, 'You come to me with a _____ and with a _____ and with a _____ , but I come to you in the _____ of the _____ of _____ , the _____ of the armies of Israel, whom you have defied.'"**

Xerxes brought all his government and military leaders to Susa. Historians believe his purpose was to build support for his plans to invade Greece. It may have been during these six months that they planned their mission to do so.

When their time together was coming to an end, the king threw a lavish, week-long feast. The party occurred in the garden of the king's palace, a celebration with expensive curtains attached to silver rods, marble pillars, and couches made of gold and silver. The floor of the garden was a pavement of "porphyry, marble, mother-of-pearl, and precious stones." The drinking vessels they used were made of gold. In the Bible, there are only two other descriptions of an elaborate building mentioned: the tabernacle (Exodus 25-28) and the temple in Jerusalem (I Kings 7). It is possible the golden drinking vessels came from the temple in Jerusalem when Nebuchadnezzar conquered it.

Everyone partied to their heart's content, with the king giving them anything and everything they wanted. He was demonstrating that he could and would reward everyone who went to battle for him against Greece.

While Xerxes was giving a feast for the men, his wife, Queen Vashti, was giving a feast for the women inside the palace.

**3** How can wealth, like power, intimidate you? Why is it harder to be courageous with a wealthy person than with a poor person? Write your answer here.

_____

_____

_____

_____

_____

_____

_____

_____

On the final day of the feast, the king was drunk, which was not a surprise. The Greek historian Herodotus stated that the Persians drank heavily when conducting government business because they believed it put them in closer touch with the spiritual world and helped them make better decisions. In his drunken state, the king called for the queen to be brought before all the men at his party.

The queen was a beautiful woman, the Bible says so. The king wanted to parade her before the men and some Jewish commentators believe the language indicates that the king wanted the queen to appear nude except for her crown. But the queen refused. She knew that her drunk husband and the inebriated men wouldn't treat her kindly. She, instead, decided against being the subject of insults and sexual harassment.

The reason for Queen Vashti's refusal isn't given in the Bible. There are two different views of why she acted the way she did. Some scholars believe that she was a rebellious woman who wanted to make a statement to the king. Others view her as a courageous woman who refused to be morally humiliated in front of her husband's friends. Knowing the consequences of disobeying the king, it appears she acted courageously rather than rebelliously.

**4**  We often think of a courageous person winning in the end. How can courage to do the right thing negatively affect the following people:

Employee who refuses to hide employer's illegal activities:

Teacher who reports child abuse in a political family:

Neighbor who reports drug activity in her community:

Person who refuses sexual advances of a date:

The king was embarrassed by Vashti's refusal. He grew angry. No one, including the queen, disobeyed his commands! He immediately asked his advisors what he should do. These advisors were called "wise men who knew the times." Persian kings usually had a council of seven men who interacted with them daily. They were among the few who could approach the king without permission. Like the wise men who sought Jesus shortly after his birth, they were astrologers who studied the stars in search of divine help. It is possible these were the type of men mentioned in Ezra 7:14 when Ezra received permission to return to Jerusalem. The king wanted to know what the law allowed or required him to do to those who disobeyed. If there was no such law, he wanted to create one.

**5**  Anger often causes quick, bad decisions. Using Proverbs 14:17 and Proverbs 16:32 as your guide, complete these two verses:

"A man of quick _____ acts _____, and a man of evil devices is hated." (Prov. 14:17 ESV)

"Whoever is _____ to anger is better than the _____, and he who rules his _____ than he who takes a city." (Prov. 16:32 ESV)

By asking his counselors what he should do, the king turned a personal issue into a national one. Memucan, one of the seven counselors, told the king that Queen Vashti offended the whole nation and not just him. Furthermore, it would affect how other women acted toward their husbands. If the women heard how the queen stood up to the king, then all women would start standing up to their husbands! Apparently, women in the kingdom admired Queen Vashti if her actions prompted a similar response.

Using this argument, Memucan and the king's advisors insisted that the king issue a "royal order" that Queen Vashti would never again be allowed in the presence of the king and that her position should be given to a "better" woman. "Better" probably meant they could find a more cooperative woman.

**6**  **In contrast to the queen's action, how did the recommendation of the king's advisors lack courage? What could they have said that would have demonstrated courage? Why do you think they chose not to courageously say what the king needed to hear instead of what he wanted to hear?**

_____

_____

_____

_____

_____

The counselors also advised the king to make the order known throughout the kingdom so that every woman "high and low alike" would respect their husband.

**7**  **The king's advisors incorrectly thought a law would make women respect their husbands. Circle the following actions that cause respect rather than a legal order.**

Public embarrassing someone                Affirming a person's worth

Listening to one's concerns                    Screaming commands

Ignoring someone                    Making another's wishes a priority

13

When the king's counselors convinced him that the decree should be issued, they immediately told him to make sure the law was sent to every province. It was to be translated and sent in every possible language so that everyone understood the law.

The Persian empire consisted of many different cultures and languages. Although Aramaic was the most understood language, translators translated it into the language of every group. Then, a well-organized group of couriers relayed the message from point to point throughout the kingdom. In a short time, everyone heard the decree of the king.

**8** Queen Vashti is never mentioned again in the book of Esther. No longer queen, she probably lived as a common person without the attention she received in the palace. She paid a high price for her courage. Have you ever regretted doing something courageous because it cost you? If so, write your feelings here:

## Further Study

Joseph was a man who courageously did the right thing but suffered for it. Read Genesis 39. What motivated Joseph to courageously do the right thing? How does his courage affect ours? How should we act and react when tempted or when we see a wrong being done?

## Journal Your Journey

# Prayer Requests

# Week Two

# Courage to Stand :
## COURAGE TO BE

"Now Esther was winning favor in the eyes of all
who saw her."

Esther 2:15b

---

Since the early days of television, there have been various shows with the purpose of contestants finding someone to date or marry. From 'The Dating Game' in the 1960s to 'The Bachelor' and 'The Bachelorette' today, relationships often are viewed as a contest with one person choosing who the date or mate will be. The idea of having a contest for finding love isn't new.

After Queen Vashti embarrassed her husband by refusing to appear before his drunken leaders and was removed from her position as queen, approximately four years passed before Esther entered the story. Most scholars believe that the king went to war against Greece but was defeated and returned home embarrassed.

It is unclear if the king's remembrance of Queen Vashti brought feelings of regret or thoughts of finding a new wife. Either way, a new queen was needed.

The young men close to the king suggested that beautiful young women from throughout the kingdom be brought to Susa, pampered, and brought before the king who would choose his next queen from among them.

This process was new, even for Persian monarchs. Normally, the queen came from the leading families in the kingdom. But this new idea pleased the king and word spread among the leaders in each province to find the most beautiful unmarried women in his area and send them to the capital.

Although it is unclear from the Scriptures, these young women probably went to Susa against their will. They had no choice, as it was an order from the king. Once a woman became a part of the king's harem, she belonged to him. Even if the king ignored her, she could never marry another man.

These young women would be in the custody of Hegai, the king's eunuch. Hegai would keep the women secluded from society for 12 months (Es. 2:12). For the first six months, the women were treated with oil of myrrh. During the final six months, the women were treated with spices and ointments. They probably ate a special diet and were taught royal etiquette as well. After one year of preparation, they would be ready to meet the king.

After she was presented to the king, each girl was put in the king's harem under the supervision of another eunuch named Shaashgaz. She could not return to her family and unless the king called for the young girl by name, she would never see him again.

**1** In a godless society like Persia, it is not surprising for women to be treated as sex objects solely to please someone in authority. How does sexism express itself in our society? Have you ever experienced it yourself?

_____

_____

_____

_____

_____

The author of Esther interrupts the story to introduce "a Jew in Susa the citadel whose name was Mordecai" (Es. 2:5). The term "Jew" originated from the word Judah and referred to any Israelite. It set apart God's people who were living in the Persian empire.

**2** As Christians, we, too, often refuse to give up some things to follow Christ. Circle some things that you have given up or changed to follow Jesus.

Relationships                    Entertainment

Employment                      Reading Materials

Sinful Habits                      Words

Although the Bible doesn't mention a wife or children, Mordecai did adopt his younger cousin. Hadassah was her Hebrew name, but she was better known by her Persian name, Esther. She was the daughter of Abihail (Es. 2:15), the uncle of Mordecai. Her mother and father died when she was young, and Mordecai, who was probably much older, reared her as his own daughter.

**3**  Adoption and foster care is a powerful way to show the love of Christ. What are some ways that you can show your love and support for people who adopt and foster children?

_____

_____

_____

_____

_____

_____

_____

When Esther is chosen as one of the young women for the king's contest, it is unclear if Mordecai arranged it or if a local leader selected her. Either way, the author noted that she "had a beautiful figure and was lovely to look at" (Es. 2:7). This probably helped her to stand out among the other women. Esther is taken away from the simple life she's always known and put into seclusion with the other contestants for an entire year. When she left for the king's harem, Mordecai told Esther not to reveal her Jewish identity (Es. 2:10). He may have feared it would prevent her from being considered for the position of queen or he may have known the feelings of some in the palace toward the Jews. Either way, Esther agreed. Every day Mordecai checked on Esther to see how she was doing.

Shortly after arriving to begin her training, Esther found favor with Hegai who was in charge. He not only provided her with the proper food and cosmetics, but he assigned seven maids to assist her and gave them the best places to stay.

**4**  God often works by putting people in our lives who "favor" us or like us. Using your Bible, list the three people who gave Esther favor.

(Esther 2:9)

(Esther 2:15)

(Esther 2:17)

The day finally came for Esther to be presented to the king. Since Hegai favored Esther and knew what the king liked, he helped her decide what she should take with her to meet the king. Robes in his favorite color, a hairstyle he really liked, or maybe his favorite meal prepared by the top chef of the palace. Whatever it was, it worked. As a result of her time with the king, he "loved Esther more than all the women" and "she won grace and favor in his sight" (Es. 2:17).

The king didn't need to see any of the remaining women. He was ready to give out his final rose, if you will. His decision was made, and the king placed the crown on Esther's head proclaiming her queen. To announce his decision, he gave a feast, declared a holiday, and gave gifts. No one had to work or pay taxes that day, so the entire citadel of Susa was celebrating.

**5** **Throughout the Book of Esther, wise people receive good advice (i.e. Mordecai to Esther, Hegai to Esther). Using your Bible, complete these two verses regarding the value of godly wisdom.**

**"Let the _____ hear and increase in learning, and the one who _____ obtain guidance." (Proverbs 1:5 ESV)**

**"The thoughts of the _____ are just; the counsels of the _____ are deceitful." (Proverbs 12:5 ESV)**

The story moves from Esther's feast to Mordecai "sitting at the king's gate" (Es. 2:19). In Persia, the king's gate was a place near the entrance to the capital city where official business took place. It was a large building where government business was transacted and business conflicts were settled. His presence in the building indicated Mordecai held some official government position. It is possible that Esther helped him obtain the position after she became queen. It certainly would allow Mordecai to see her more often.

While conducting his duties, Mordecai learns that two men, Bigthan and Teresh, are plotting to kill the king. The men guarded the king's assets, but were angry and planning to assassinate him. The reason for their anger isn't given. It is possible they were upset about Esther becoming queen. Traditionally, the king selected his queen from one of the seven noble families in the kingdom. Because people with access to the king often accepted bribes for favors, they could be upset with Vashti being dethroned. Queen Vashti may have done favors for the men.

Mordecai told Esther what he knew. Queen Esther, in turn, told the king and gave all the credit to Mordecai for reporting it. Xerxes investigated and found it was true. He immediately ordered the men to be hung "on the gallows" (Es. 2:23). The Hebrew word translated "gallows" meant a tree. It probably meant they were impaled on a stake, one of the more common means of capital punishment in Persia.

Mordecai demonstrated his courage by telling Queen Esther about the plot. The king could have dismissed what he said and ordered Mordecai to be killed, and Esther too, but God was working through Mordecai and Queen Esther to fulfill His plan.

 **What is the difference between gossip and reporting the truth to help? Circle the actions that demonstrate a proper reason for telling someone what you know.**

So everyone will know        So they can intervene

So they can pray        So they can laugh at someone

So they can encourage        So they can get ahead

The king recorded the events, including the role of Mordecai, in the "book of the chronicles". Historians note that kings often kept an official record of what happened in their kingdom. Persian kings often kept an official list of people whose actions demonstrated their loyalty to the king. Normally, the king always rewarded someone who helped him or showed loyalty to him. The king, however, didn't reward Mordecai immediately. Mordecai may have been disappointed, but, God was working even then.

**7** Many people are disappointed when they aren't recognized for their good deeds. How do you respond? Read Matthew 19:27-30. How did Jesus respond to Peter when Peter asked how he would be rewarded for following Jesus?

_____

_____

_____

_____

_____

_____

_____

_____

_____

# Further Study

For Further Study: Esther didn't refuse the food and cosmetics offered her by the king. Read Daniel 1:8-21. Daniel and the three young Hebrew boys, also captives in Persia, did. When is it wise to stand against governmental authority? When is it not? What should govern a Christian's actions and interactions with government officials?

# Journal Your Journey

# Prayer Requests

# Week Three

# Courage to Stand :
## COURAGE TO STAND

"...But Mordecai did not bow down or pay homage."

Esther 3:2b

---

In 2006, a young college football player named Tim Tebow became a national sensation when his University of Florida team won the NCAA National Football Championship. Tebow was a humble young man who won the respect of thousands. His popularity only increased when he became the first sophomore to win the Heisman Trophy in 2017 and lead his team to a second national championship in 2008. Tebow was a vocal Christian who became famous for kneeling on the field to pray, a practice that became known as "tebowing".

Although a gracious young man, Tebow also became known for his moral convictions that contradicted the accepted norm of his day. In particular, he expressed his belief in sexual abstinence until marriage and committed to marrying as a virgin. Although he was criticized, Tim Tebow won the respect of many for verbalizing and living his convictions. God honors those who stand for their biblical convictions.

The third chapter of Esther begins by introducing a new personality, a man named Haman. Haman is identified as an Agagite and the son of Hammedatha. Being an Agagite probably meant that Haman was a descendent of Agag, the king of the Amalekites. This probably explains Haman's hatred of the Jews and Mordecai's disrespect for him.

Agag was the king of the Amalekites when Saul was the king of Israel. (I Sam. 15). The Amalekites lived in a desert region and were descendants of Amalek, the grandson of Esau. They were under God's judgment because they attacked the Israelites before they entered the Promised Land. As a result, God promised Moses that He would destroy the Amalekites (Ex. 17:8-16).

When Saul became king, God commanded him through Samuel the prophet for the Israelites to destroy the Amalekites and everything associated with them. Saul did attack but refused to kill everyone, including their king, Agag (I Sam. 15:1-3). As a result, the Amalekites continued to fight with the Israelites for many years.

**1** Disobeying God, Saul kept Agag, the king of the Amalekites, alive and kept the best of their possessions. Read I Samuel 15:10-15. How did Saul try to make his disobedience sound like he was doing something spiritual? How do we often do the same thing? Can you think of an example from your own life where you tried to rationalize your disobedience?

_____

_____

_____

_____

_____

_____

_____

_____

_____

_____

_____

_____

From the time Esther became the queen of Persia to the opening verses of chapter three, approximately five years passed. During that time, the king promoted a man named Haman to be over all the government officials, including Mordecai. No reason is given for the promotion, but it appears Haman actively sought the position and possibly manipulated the king into giving it to him. With his new role, the king ordered that everyone must bow to Haman when they were in his presence, much like a modern soldier is ordered to salute a commanding officer.

Mordecai refused to bow. No reason is given, but it was probably due to Mordecai being a Jew. It is during this time that Mordecai reveals his nationality to the other government leaders. The Jews and the Agagites (Amalekites) despised each other and Jews would not pay respect to a pagan. For Mordecai, it may have been more personal because he was of the tribe of Benjamin, the same tribe as King Saul.

The government leaders tried to reason with Mordecai, but he continued to refuse to bow when Haman came into his presence. Finally, the other government leaders reported it to Haman. Instead of dealing with Mordecai personally, Haman decided to trick the king into killing all the Jews in the kingdom.

**2** **Read Proverbs 6:16-19 and list the seven things God hates. As you continue to see the actions of Haman, how do you think God felt about them?**

1. _____

2. _____

3. _____

4. _____

5. _____

6. _____

7. _____

Haman knew he could flatter the king and get what he wanted: an order for all Jews to be killed. First, Haman had to set a time for the order to be carried out. People in the East rarely did anything without consulting the stars or omens. One of their favorite ways to determine when to do something was to cast "pur." Pur was the Persian name for lots. The lots were clay cubes with numbers or drawings on them. We often associate dice with gambling or games, but the ancients used dice to determine divine direction.

It is interesting to note that Haman cast the lots during the month of Nisan, the time corresponding to Jewish Passover. While God isn't mentioned in the book of Esther, it is clear to see the Satanic influence in Haman's actions. Jehovah promised the Jews a Messiah. If all the Jews were killed, no Messiah could come. But God was working behind the scenes to accomplish His will.

**3** Read Psalm 132:11. Complete the verse below that states the promise of a coming Messiah in the Old Testament.

"The Lord_____ to David, a sure oath from which He will not _____ _____ : "One of the sons of your body I will set on your _____." (Psalm 132:11 ESV)

The month of Adar, the twelfth month on the Babylonian calendar, was the time the lots set for Haman to ask for the killing of the Jews. That meant Haman had to wait 12 months to see his desire accomplished! His superstition, however, would not permit him to request any other time. Even with the lots, God was at work giving Mordecai, Esther, and the Jews 12 months to plan their intervention.

To persuade the king to make the law, Haman lied about what was happening and how the king could prosper from it. First, he told the king that a group of "certain people" were refusing to obey the laws. They were rebelling against the king. The Jews weren't rebelling. Jeremiah instructed the Jews while living in a foreign land to obey the law. (Jer. 29:4-7). Only Mordecai was refusing to obey one law, the law that required him to bow in Haman's presence. But Haman's anger caused him to exaggerate and blame all the Jews.

**4** Pride and anger cause people to seek revenge and lie to make it happen. Has there been a time when you observed someone seeking revenge? Write your feelings about it here.

Every king fears a rebellion. Haman knew that accusing the Jews of disobeying the law would prompt the king to agree to their destruction. It is interesting to note that Haman never mentioned the Jews. He referred to them as "a certain people scattered abroad" (Es. 3:8). And the king never asked who the people were.

The first part of Haman's appeal was to the king's power. The second part was to his greed. Haman promised 10,000 talents of silver would come to the king's treasury, almost 375 tons of silver! Historians estimate that Haman promised the king a reward equal to two-thirds of the total annual income from taxes. The king's wealth declined greatly in his failed attempt to conquer Greece, and Haman knew it. He probably thought this money would come from taking everything the Jews had when they were killed. The king declined the offer of money, an Oriental custom of the time, but he probably knew it would be given to him anyway.

The threat of a rebellion and the promise of money prompted the king to issue the decree that all Jews must die. To ensure it, he gave his signet ring to Haman. Kings in ancient times didn't sign documents as proof they authorized them. Instead, they used a signet ring to seal the document. By giving Haman the ring, the king gave him royal authority. The author noted that Haman was "the enemy of the Jews." (Es. 3:10)

 **People often use manipulation to get their way. Circle the negative effects of someone using manipulation and half-lies.**

| | |
|---|---|
| Trust is destroyed | They gain friends |
| They get what they want | They please God |
| They become selfish | People manipulate them |

The author of the book of Esther goes into detail to show the extent Haman went to make sure everyone knew about the decree. He immediately called the king's scribes together to get the message out. These scribes were individuals who acted as clerks to reproduce copies. Since Haman approached the king in the "first month, which is the month of Nisan" and summoned the scribes on the thirteenth, he was motivated to announce the law as soon as possible. The thirteenth also was the day before Passover.

Haman wanted a copy sent to every satrap, governor, and noble under the king's authority. A satrap was the ruler over one of twenty divisions in the kingdom. The governors headed smaller divisions within each satrap and the nobles served under the governors. Most of the nobles were over a group of people, usually people who came from a conquered nation.

Haman not only wanted everyone to know about the law, but he also wanted everyone to understand it. He ordered the scribes to write a copy for every province and in every language. Haman wanted the Jews specifically to hear the decree in their own language. In his mind, waiting 12 months for their death would be a just repayment for the way Mordecai offended him.

 **6**

**Haman reacted to Mordecai in the wrong way. How are we as Christians to react when insulted? Using I Peter 3:9 and I Thessalonians 5:15, complete these verses to find out how we should respond.**

"Do not repay_____ for_____ or _____ for _____ , but on the contrary, _____, for to this you were called, that you may obtain a _____." (I Pt. 3:9 ESV)

"See that no one repays anyone_____ for _____, but always seek to do _____ to one another and to _____ ." (I Thess. 5:15 ESV)

Once the letters containing the new law were completed, couriers took them to every part of the kingdom and delivered them to the appropriate official. The law and the instructions were clear: they were to "destroy, to kill and annihilate all Jews" (Es. 3:13). This meant every Jew, regardless of age, including women and children. In addition, the leaders were to take everything the Jews owned when they killed them. The officials who received the proclamation had the responsibility to tell every person under their authority.

The couriers obeyed. Each leader received their copy with the order to kill the Jews on the appointed day 12 months later. The Bible doesn't record how all the Jews responded, but based on Mordecai's response in Esther 4:1, it is possible they wept. Why would they not? The laws of the Medes and Persians could not be altered.

Haman, Xerxes, and the citizens in the capital had different reactions. Haman and the king had a drink (Es. 3:15). Haman was probably happy to be getting even with Mordecai and the Jews. The king, on the other hand, probably didn't think much about the decision to kill the Jews. For him, it was putting down a rebellion.

The city of Susa, however, reacted with confusion. The citizens knew there was no uprising happening in the kingdom. Most of them probably had Jewish friends and knew they were not a threat to the king. But the citizens, like the Jews, were powerless against the decrees of their government.

## Further Study

Read Matthew 6:1-14. As Christians, how are our actions and reactions to be different from unbelievers? What does Jesus teach about our willingness to forgive? How does forgiveness or our refusal to forgive affect our prayer life? Our relationships?

## Journal Your Journey

# Prayer Requests

# Week Four

# Courage to Stand :
## COURAGE TO INTERCEDE

"...And who knows whether you have not come to the kingdom for such a time as this?"

Esther 4:14b

---

You could not believe what you were seeing on the evening news. A sweet, elderly lady just a few blocks from your home was robbed, assaulted, and left for dead. The main suspect is a young man who was desperate for money to buy drugs. A few weeks later, you learn there have been several break-ins and police believe they are drug-related as well. You think something must be done!

You contact elected officials, coordinate with your neighbors to report any suspicious behavior, and resolve to stand firm against the drug lords who are trying to take your community.

Then, you get a major promotion at work. Your income increases dramatically and you buy your dream home in a better neighborhood. Then the mayor calls. He wants to appoint you to a task force to address the crime issues in your old neighborhood. You asked for some time to think about it and promised to give the mayor an answer in a few days.

Friday approaches. You want to help your former neighbors, but it will be risky. What if the drug lords target you, your family, and your home for revenge? What if your life becomes endangered? What if people avoid you because of your stand?

The response is easy to make in a hypothetical world but being willing to risk your life, your possessions, and your position isn't as easy as it appears. If you don't believe it, ask Esther.

The decree to kill all Jews in the Persian kingdom on a set day grieved all the Jews, especially Mordecai. He responded by tearing his clothes, putting on a sackcloth, and putting ashes on his head. This response was common among Jews in the Bible. It was a sign of repentance (Neh. 9:1-3) or severe grief (II Sam. 1:1-10). For Mordecai, it was a sign of grief. He, his family, and his friends were doomed to execution. Furthermore, the Jewish people would cease to exist. Hope was gone.

Mordecai went to the entrance of the king's palace wearing the sackcloth and ashes. If he was wearing normal clothes, he could enter. But the king prohibited anything unpleasant or disturbing to be near his palace. In addition, he didn't allow people to bring him bad news. As a result, the king lived isolated from reality. For him, the best way to deal with problems was to ignore them.

**1** Ignoring the struggles of others is easy to do, especially if you refuse to see or hear about them. Look over this list. How do people avoid these issues rather than addressing them? What are some other issues that you would add to this list?

Homelessness

Children in poverty

Drugs/Crime

Historians estimate nearly 15 million Jews lived in the Persian kingdom when the king made this decree. They reacted like Mordecai, with weeping and wearing sackcloth. The Jews living in the capital heard the news first, and over the next several months, Jews throughout the kingdom would hear the law read and know they had a limited number of days to live.

Mordecai probably came near the entrance to the king's palace so people associated with Esther would see him. He wanted to attract attention so he could get a message to Esther.

The attendants that were assigned to Esther reported what Mordecai was doing. It is unclear why they told the queen, but they may have known of their relationship. Queen Esther didn't inquire about the reasons for Mordecai's behavior. Instead, she sent clothes to Mordecai. He refused to accept them.

Now Esther knew something was seriously wrong. She sent Hathach, one of the eunuchs assigned by the king to care for the queen, to talk with Mordecai. Mordecai told him about Haman's plot. He specifically reported the amount of money Haman promised the king for destroying the Jews. It is uncertain how Mordecai knew about the money. Knowing the arrogance of Haman, he probably bragged about it publicly.

Mordecai knew the message he needed to convey to Queen Esther. To be sure she believed him, he gave Hathach a copy of the decree to read for herself.
As the queen, she was isolated from knowing the laws that were made and how they affected people. So Mordecai not only gave her a copy of the law, but he also sent a personal plea for Esther to beg the king to save "her people" (Es. 3:8).

Mordecai announced earlier in the story that he was a Jew (Es. 3:4). If the people in the king's palace didn't know Esther was Jewish, they found out when Mordecai revealed it to Hathach. Some scholars think Hathach also may have been a Jew since Jewish people often worked in the king's palace. Either way, Mordecai knew Haman would discover his kinship to Esther and make the connection that she, too, was one of the people to be killed by his decree.

**2** **God's plan often includes people that appear insignificant. Hathach didn't realize the important role he played. Throughout the Bible, God often used people whose names aren't mentioned. Read the following verses and note what the "unnamed" person(s) did that seemed insignificant but played a big role in God's plan.**

**Servant Girl (II Kings 5: 1-14)**

**Men on the roof (Mark 2: 1-5)**

**Woman (Mark 14: 3-9)**

Esther probably wanted to honor Mordecai's request, but there was one major problem. She didn't know how or when she could discuss it with the king. The law stated that no one could go into the king's presence without being requested or being granted an invitation. If someone tried to access the king without permission, they were killed immediately.

According to the historian Herodotus, an earlier king named Deioces the Mede, made this law and it continued in force. If you wanted to see the king, you told one of the eunuchs who served as his messengers. They, in turn, told the king. The king could ignore or grant your request. Only a small group of advisors could approach the king regularly without permission. Haman was one of them. Queen Esther was not.

There was one exception to the law. If you approached the king and he extended his golden scepter, your life was spared, and you could talk with him. But was it worth the risk?

Esther explains to Mordecai through Hathach that she had not been in the presence of the king for a month. After five years as queen, the king didn't call for her as often as he once did. While Esther may have been willing to ask the king, approaching him didn't appear to be an option.

**3** **At this point, Esther wasn't willing to take a step of faith and trust God for the results. Complete this verse:**

"_____ is the assurance of things _____ for, the conviction of things not _____". (Hebrews 11:1)

Mordecai doesn't back down but presses his case with a personal appeal. He reminds Esther, just as she wasn't exempt from being killed by approaching the king without permission, that she wasn't exempt from being killed as a Jew. The law didn't exempt any Jew – man, woman, child, or queen! In other words, it wasn't just a favor for others. Esther would be saving her own life. With Haman's hatred of the Jewish people, he would ensure every Jew, including Esther, died.

Mordecai also made a second plea. He was inviting Esther to be the person God used to bring deliverance. He told her "if you keep silent at this time, relief and deliverance will rise for the Jews from another place, but you and your father's house will perish" (Es. 4:14). Mordecai remembered the covenant God made with Abraham (Gen. 12:1-3). God would not forget the Jews and they would not be destroyed from the face of the earth.

If Esther didn't act, God would deliver the Jews another way, but she and her family would perish.

Mordecai's third appeal was a reminder of the way God brought her to the throne. Long before she became queen, God was working in her life. He put Mordecai in her life to care for her when her parents died and gave her favor with government officials. In other words, God put her in the position of queen to save His people. That is why Mordecai asks Esther, "who knows whether you have not come to the kingdom for such a time as this?" (Es. 4:14).

**4** Mordecai was trying to eliminate any excuses Esther might think were valid. Circle the ones that you think might have gone through her mind. Then consider which of these excuses you have used when you saw a need.

Let someone else do it                     This is not the time

I am too busy                                      It's too risky

I can't give up my lifestyle                  I might fail

When Hathach returned with Mordecai's message, she immediately agreed and decided to do as he asked. "I will go to the king, though it is against the law, and if I perish, I perish" (Esther 4:16). But the timing was essential. The king's moods could change any time and since she hadn't been around him, she would not know in advance how he was feeling when the moment came to ask him to spare the Jews.

Esther told Mordecai to get all the Jews in Susa to fast for three days and three nights. They were to avoid eating or drinking anything. Fasting was a common practice among Jews when they were facing an impossible situation.

Avoiding food didn't guarantee a miracle or that God would act. It had to be sincere, along with humbling themselves. Many of these Jews probably knew of the fasting and humbling mentioned by Ezra (Ezra 8:21-23). Although prayer is not mentioned, it probably was included (Dan. 9:1-5).

The queen would also do her part. She fasted and she got her attendants to join her as well. These Gentile women probably loved Esther and saw the threat she faced. Their participation was essential to preventing someone from thinking that Esther was refusing to eat because she was ill.

Esther assured Mordecai that she was committed to doing as he asked. She would approach the king, even though it was illegal, and try to get him to spare the Jews. She knew the risk, but her decision was made. If she died, she died.

When there is a need, it takes courage to go against the odds. Esther had so many things against her. The king had ignored her for a month. The law prevented her from approaching the king without permission. Being a woman didn't help because the king didn't hold women in high esteem. Haman certainly would do anything to prevent the king from changing his mind.

But Esther found the strength to intercede.

**5** Like Esther, believers often face obstacles while doing what needs to be done for God's glory and the good of others. Yet, we have a promise. Complete the following verse to discover God's promise to every Christian who is willing to follow Him and courageously stand against evil.

"What then shall we _____ to these things? If_____ is for us, who can be_____ us?" (Romans 8:31)

## Further Study

Hebrews 11 contains a list of people who acted on faith. Read this chapter and make a list of the people mentioned. By the name of each one, write what they did that involved faith. Include what they did and didn't know, who was opposing them, and what things could have discouraged them. Then, make a list of things you sense God is wanting you to do that require a step of faith. Ask God to help you act as Esther and those listed in Hebrews 11 did.

# Journal Your Journey

# Prayer Requests

# Week Five

# Courage to Stand :
## COURAGE TO WAIT

"...let the king and Haman come to the feast that I will prepare for them, and tomorrow I will do as the king has said."

Esther 5:8

---

You look at your calendar for the next few weeks and there in bold letters, are your favorite words: "Vacation at the Beach." You and your family anxiously look forward every year to the sunshine and relaxation that a beach vacation brings. You find yourself uttering the words, "I just can't wait!"

You also notice two weeks before your vacation another notation: "Root canal with Doctor Johnson." The excitement over the vacation evaporates immediately. There is nothing fun about a root canal. It is painful and uncomfortable. You find yourself uttering words again, but this time you say, "I wish I could hurry up and get this over with!"

Two experiences – one pleasant and one unpleasant – prompted the same response. With one, you want to rush time to get to the beach. The sooner the fun begins, the better. With the other one, you want to get it over so you don't have to dread it.

In some ways, Esther probably experienced both emotions.  The Bible doesn't tell us how Esther felt during the three days of fasting. We don't know if she was anxious or excited. Nor do we know if she slept well the night before or experienced insomnia.

**1** How do you think Esther felt? How would you feel if you were Esther? Why?

_____

_____

_____

_____

_____

_____

_____

_____

_____

_____

_____

When the three days of fasting ended, Esther dressed in her royal robes and entered the king's throne room. The moment of truth came when the king saw her. Would he receive her with open arms or demand her execution for entering without permission?

Esther "won favor in his sight". That is, he received her into his presence. The king extended his golden scepter toward her. Esther approached him and touched the tip of the scepter.

For the first time in the book of Esther, the king referred to her as Queen Esther. He first wanted to know why she came into his presence. Obviously, the reason was important to her. The king immediately followed that question with a desire to know her request.

To set her mind at ease, the king told Esther that he would honor any request up to giving her half of his kingdom. This expression wasn't to be taken literally. It would be similar to us telling someone we would do anything in the world for them.

You would expect Esther to tell the king what she desired, but she didn't. Instead, she wanted the king and Haman to come to a feast that she prepared for them. It would be in her living quarters and only the three of them would be present. The king immediately called for Haman to come and go with them to the feast, honoring the request of the queen.

It is unclear why Esther included Haman. If the queen was alone with the king, she could present her request in private. Yet, it is possible Esther knew how the king felt about Haman and she needed an opportunity to change his feelings toward him first. In particular, Esther needed the Lord to work on the heart of the king.

While they were eating and drinking wine, the king asked Esther again what she wanted. He repeated his willingness to give her anything she wanted, up to half his kingdom.

Esther didn't feel the time was right. Esther told the king that she wanted him and Haman to return the next day for another feast and she would disclose her request then. This was an unusual act because kings always got what they wanted when they wanted it.

**2**  **Look at the list below. Circle some of the reasons that Esther may have delayed telling the king her request.**

Time wasn't right                    Didn't feel loved by the king

Something the king said          Wanted Haman to bring up the law

Haman was listening                 She thought of her plans in advance

Mordecai didn't advise her       She wanted the king to ask again

Esther's reasons for delaying the request aren't given. How the feast affected the king isn't known, but the Bible tells us how it affected Haman. Haman felt highly privileged to be the guest of the king and queen for a private dinner. He left "joyful and glad of heart." But his heart was also filled with pride.

As he returned to the palace, Haman saw Mordecai at the king's gate. Mordecai wasn't wearing the sackcloth but was dressed normally. Feeling his importance, Haman probably thought Mordecai now knew the power he possessed. As a result, he was surprised when Mordecai did not stand nor did he tremble in his presence. This is the first mention of someone trembling in Haman's presence, but it may imply the way some people feared him.

Because Mordecai refused to show him respect, Haman became angry. He probably wanted to lash out or ordered Mordecai immediately put to death. But Haman didn't. He went home and called for his friends and his wife to come to the house. He wanted to brag about being with the king and queen for a private dinner and to express his anger toward Mordecai.

When they arrived at his house, the bragging began. He "recounted" (Es. 5:11) to them how rich he was, how many sons he had, all the promotions the king gave him, and how he was second in command of the kingdom. Haman probably gained his riches by dishonest means.

According to Esther 9:7-10, Haman had 10 sons. Persian society valued men with many sons. Furthermore, the positions the king gave him made him politically powerful.

Haman probably felt smart and superior to other people. He told his wife and friends that the queen seemed to like him as much as the king. After all, only he was invited to dine privately with the king and queen in the queen's living quarters. No one in all the kingdom had experienced what he did. He was special in the eyes of royalty. The message the proud Haman conveyed to his wife and friends was how honored they should be to know him!

**3** **Pride is a powerful, destructive force. The Bible lists pride ("haughty eyes") first as the things God hates (Prov. 6:16-19). Complete these verses from the Book of Proverbs to see the danger of having a proud heart.**

"_____ goes before _____ , and a haughty spirit before a _____ ." (Proverbs 16:18)

"One's _____ will bring him _____ , but he who is _____ in spirit will obtain _____ ." (Proverbs 29:23)

Esther knew that Haman was a proud man. Whether she knew how it was affecting Haman or not, the queen would use his pride to her advantage. She probably knew Haman's pride would prevent him from seeing her plan to save the Jews. Based on her experience with proud people, she also probably knew that it would cause his destruction.

After Haman bragged to his wife and friends about his achievements, he revealed how mad he was because Haman refused to stand and tremble when he walked by him. His hurt feelings revealed his insecurity.

Though he had wealth, sons, and political power, Haman was obsessed with Mordecai's disrespect toward him. Money, family, and power weren't enough. He wanted Mordecai out of his sight. He couldn't stand seeing him at the king's gate every day. Haman said everything else didn't mean anything to him as long as Mordecai kept embarrassing him.

**4** Boasting associated with pride is the danger of malice. Malice is a desire to hurt someone who hurt us. It is the opposite of forgiveness. Read I Corinthians 6:6-8. How was the boasting of the Corinthians, malice, and evil connected? What did Paul compare malice to? What do Paul's words teach us about the importance of forgiveness?

**5** Zeresh's words and suggestion resembled another Old Testament woman, Jezebel. Read I Kings 21:1-16. How did the actions of Jezebel resemble the actions of Zeresh?

Their plan was for Haman to build "gallows fifty cubits high" and "in the morning tell the king to have Mordecai hanged upon it" (Es. 5:14). It is unclear from the original Hebrew if the gallows referred to a platform for hanging, like capital punishment in the early days of the United States, or to a long pole a person could be attached to. Based on historical records, it probably was a long pole with a stake driven through the person's body.

Persians loved making people suffer when putting them to death. With Haman's hatred for Mordecai, he wanted to see Mordecai suffer before he died.
The pole was "fifty cubits high" or 75 feet high. The height would be excessive if it was a single pole. Haman probably attached the pole to the wall of the city or the roof of a building. It was important to Haman for the people to see Mordecai suffering and dying.

To illustrate how cold-hearted Haman, his wife, and his friends were, they suggested that he "go joyfully with the king to the feast" with Queen Esther after Mordecai was on the gallows. Pride and malice think revenge would bring joy, but it doesn't.

## Further Study

Throughout Esther, there is an emphasis on the inability of a person to approach the king, the danger of doing so uninvited, and how a person would approach the king if permitted to speak with him. Study Hebrews 4:14-16. How are believers to approach their Heavenly Father, the King of Kings? What emotions should a Christian experience as he prays? Make a list of the differences between approaching our King and the king in the Book of Esther.

# Journal Your Journey

# Prayer Requests

# Week Six

**6**

# Courage to Stand :
## COURAGE TO SPEAK

"Then King Ahasuerus said to Queen Esther, 'Who is he, and where is he, who has dared to do this? And Esther said, 'A foe and enemy! This wicked Haman!"

Esther 7:5-6

---

It is every parent's nightmare. Your child comes home from school, goes to their room, isn't interested in eating dinner, and is extremely quiet. You know something is wrong.

When you ask if something is wrong, they reply, "No!" But your parental instincts tell you differently.

You probe further. You promise a reward if they will tell you what is worrying them. Still, no answers.

Then, you start asking questions and gauge their responses. Were they sick? Did they make a bad grade? Did a teacher punish them for doing something wrong? Every question resulted in your child shaking their head to tell you "no."

After a few moments you ask, "Is someone bullying you at school?" Tears fill their eyes as they try to muster the courage to tell you, "Yes." But they don't have to tell you, you already know.

After assuring them of your love and concern, they tell you about a bigger kid at school who makes fun of them, demands they do things for them, and constantly embarrasses them. As a parent, you want to go to the school and address the problem. But you know if you do, your child will be disappointed and wounded by your actions.

You wait and pray for the opportunity to address the situation. Eventually, the day comes and you deal with the issue. Timing is important because you need to be controlled by reason rather than emotion. And timing is important because you need to make sure that the person empowered to address it is open to receiving your message.

 **Bullies can be adults too. Circle the ways you have observed bullies hurting other people.**

Shaming someone          Physically harming someone

Embarrassing someone          Mocking a disability

Calling someone names          Threatening someone

Haman was a bully of the worst kind. As the second in command, Haman had the power to bully people and harm them. Because Mordecai refused to bow before him, Haman plotted how he could hang Mordecai on the gallows for everyone to see. Months later, all the Jews would be killed and people, Haman thought, would fear and respect him.

Like the earlier events in the book of Esther, God is working behind the scenes to protect the Jews. After the first banquet with Queen Esther, Haman returned to his house and went to bed. The king, however, could not sleep.

No reason is given for the king's insomnia. Maybe he was worried about the financial condition of his kingdom, or maybe something he ate was keeping him awake. Whatever the reason, God had a role in it.

Unable to sleep, the king ordered the "book of memorable deeds, the chronicles" (Es. 6:1) be read to him. The king probably thought the reading would help him go to sleep. This book was an official diary of the king. It contained records of events that were important. In it were the names of people who helped the king and how he rewarded them for their loyalty. Because the safety of the king and his kingdom depended on people being loyal, rewarding people was very important.

One by one, the king heard of helpful and heroic events and how he rewarded the people. Then he gets to the part about Mordecai telling the king about the plot of Bigthana and Teresh (see Es. 2:19-23). When the king asked how Mordecai was rewarded, he was told that nothing was done.

The king was upset. Failing to reward Mordecai meant that he might fail to report another assassination plot. But Mordecai wasn't upset and continued serving in the kingdom. Now, God was going to use the oversight to reward Mordecai, destroy Haman, and save the Jews.

 **People often get their feelings hurt when they aren't recognized for their actions and it is compounded when others are recognized. Has there been a time when you were hurt because someone didn't acknowledge your service? How did it affect your spiritual walk? How has the Lord used that experience to teach you a spiritual truth? Write your answers on the next page.**

_____

_____

_____

_____

_____

Although it was late in the night, the king wanted someone to suggest a way to honor Mordecai for revealing the assassination plot five years earlier. He asked who was in the royal court. When he heard that Haman was there, he called for him to come into his bedroom.

It is unclear why Haman was in the royal court during the night. He possibly wanted to be there when the king got up to get him to order the execution of Mordecai. Although Haman was one of the few to have access to the king, it was a high honor to be asked to come into the king's bedroom.

Without any explanation, the king asked Haman what should be done for the man the king wishes to honor. Haman, proud and self-centered, believed the king was going to honor him. He couldn't ask for a promotion because he already was the second in the land. He didn't ask for money because he already was a wealthy man. Haman suggested that the man wear the king's robe and crest while riding the king's horse through town.

Can you imagine the surprise when the king told Haman that he liked the idea and to honor Mordecai in the way he suggested? Though he held a powerful position, Haman could not refuse a direct order from the king. Humiliated, Haman dressed Mordecai in the king's robe and led him through the city riding the king's horse.

**3** **Haman and Mordecai illustrate Proverbs 29:23. After completing the verse here, draw a circle around the phrase that illustrates Haman and a square around the one that illustrates Mordecai.**

**"One's_____ will bring him _____, but he who is _____ in spirit will obtain _____."**
**(Prov. 29:23 ESV)**

After leading the horse with Mordecai riding it through the city, Haman had to return the horse, remove the royal robes, and return Mordecai to the city gate. Mordecai, who had a humble spirit, felt honored by the king's actions. Haman, however, felt humiliated.

Haman returned home with his head covered. Covering one's head was a sign of mourning and grieving. Mordecai did it (see Es. 4:1-2) when he heard of the law to destroy the Jews. In addition to mourning, it could be a response to embarrassment. Haman's actions probably indicated both.

When he arrived home, his wife, Zeresh, and all his friends knew that Haman was upset. He told them everything that happened. This time, instead of giving him advice and trying to cheer him up, they warned him that he was doomed.

Until now, Haman didn't tell his family and friends that Mordecai was Jewish. Now that they knew, their advice changed. Persians were superstitious people who believed when bad things happened, more bad things followed. It is possible they remembered how God made promises to the Jewish people.

The last thing Haman wanted to do was show his face in public. But while he was talking with his wife and friends, the king's eunuchs arrived to take him to the banquet at Queen Esther's home. The added phrase "hurried to bring Haman to the feast" (Es. 6:14) might imply that Haman forgot about the engagement.

**4** **How and where we get advice is very important. Why do you think Haman's wife and friends were quick to give him advice on how to get rid of Mordecai? (see Es. 5:9-14) Why do you think their comments changed when they heard how Haman was humiliated?**

Haman and the king feasted with Queen Esther, just as they did the day before. The "second day" (Es. 7:2) doesn't refer to two days of feasting but shows it was at the second banquet that she gave for them. The king repeated his desire to know what Queen Esther wanted from him. He again promised, "even to the half of my kingdom, it shall be fulfilled" (Es. 7:2). This phrase, as in Esther 5:3, wasn't to be taken literally but implied how willing he was to give her what she wanted.

The moment had arrived for Queen Esther to ask the king to spare the Jews. Esther placed her life and the Jews, "her people" (Es. 7:4) together. To do something for her, meant the king had to do it for all the Jews. This was the first time that the king and Haman heard that the queen was Jewish.

Before the king could respond, Queen Esther continued. She quoted from the decree that he signed ordering the murder of all the Jews (see Es. 3:13). The king learned that the Jews were being murdered to get their possessions. If instead, the king had decided to sell them as slaves for money, the queen said that she would not have troubled the king with her request.

The king found the unfortunate situation hard to believe. He immediately wanted to know what evil person caused him to sign the decree.

Subjects viewed a Persian king as a god. In their minds, the king could not make a mistake. As a result, Persian kings always blamed someone for their mistakes. That is why he asked, "Who is he, and where is he, who has dared to do this?" (Es. 7:5).

Esther told the king that it was Haman who did it. The news terrified Haman. He knew that he immediately lost his standing and influence with the king.

**5** **Queen Esther courageously spoke for the Jews. Who are some people in your community that lack a voice that you can speak for? How can you do it?**

_____

_____

_____

_____

_____

_____

The king had a short temper. He left the room angry and went to the palace garden. Haman should have left too, but he knew that the king would kill him. So, he stayed behind to beg Queen Esther to intercede for him and to ask the king to spare his life.

Persian custom stated that only the king could be left alone with the queen or any woman in his harem. No man could get within seven steps of a woman that belonged to the king. When Haman fell onto Esther who was sitting on a couch to beg for his life, he violated both customs.

When the king returned and saw what Haman was doing, he expressed his anger. Before he could finish speaking, the king's servants covered Haman's face. Earlier, Haman covered his face in humiliation. Now the king's servant's covered his face in preparation for his execution.

Harbona, one of the eunuchs holding Haman, remembered the gallows Haman constructed to kill Mordecai. He suggested they use them for the death of Haman. The king ordered the servants to execute him.

With the death of Haman, "the wrath of the king abated" (Es. 7:10). The word "abated" is the same Hebrew word used in Genesis 8:1 for the waters receding after the Flood.

**6** **The king wasn't without fault. Reflecting on this and the previous studies, make a list of mistakes the king made.**

## Further Study

Read Galatians 6:7 and Numbers 32:23. How does this statement apply to Haman? What other Bible characters found this to be true? Here are some verses to explore for hints: Adam and Eve (Genesis 3); Samson (Judges 16); David (II Samuel 11). How did their sins affect them spiritually and physically? How did it affect their influence, their character, and their families?

## Journal Your Journey

# Prayer Requests

# Week Seven

# Courage to Stand :
## COURAGE TO RESCUE

"Then Mordecai went out from the presence of the
king in royal robes of blue and white, with a great
golden crown and a robe of fine linen and purple, and
the city of Susa shouted and rejoiced."

Esther 8:15

---

In almost every legislative election, there is a newcomer to politics who promises to
address issues and make necessary changes for the better. They organize committees,
advertise, and publicly campaign. Then, they get elected. Shortly after taking office,
the newly elected legislator discovers that it is easier to get elected than it is to
change a law.

Edicts issued by a Persian king could not be changed. The law stood forever. The only
possible solution was for the king to issue a new law, one that would neutralize the old
one.

Before discussing a new law, the king wanted to make things right with Queen Esther.
Whenever a traitor was executed, his estate was confiscated by the king. The king
normally kept the traitor's possessions for himself. In this case, the king gave Haman's
wealth to Queen Esther.

Queen Esther told the king about her blood relationship with Mordecai. Earlier, the
king learned that Esther was a Jew, just like Mordecai. Now he knows they are related.
It is possible that she also told the king about Mordecai adopting her as a young girl
when her father and mother died (see Es. 2:8).

The king had to replace Haman's position in the government. Remembering how loyal Mordecai was in revealing the plot to kill the king (see Es. 2:19-23) and how he was related to Esther, Xerxes gave Mordecai the powerful position that Haman held.

Mordecai became the second in command of the whole kingdom. By giving him his signet ring, Mordecai had the power to issue decrees and laws in the name of the king.

Upon receiving this honor, Queen Esther gave Mordecai the estate of Haman that was given to her. In less than 24 hours, Mordecai went from being a humble servant of the king destined to die on the gallows to a wealthy man that was second in command of the Persian Empire!

**1** The Bible is filled with promises that God will reward the godly and destroy the wicked. It may not happen as quickly or in the way we desire, but His promises are true. Use Psalm 37:37-38 to complete these verses and see this promise of God:

"Mark the _____ and behold the _____, for there is a future for the man of_____ . But transgressors shall be altogether_____, the future of the _____ shall be cut off." (Psalm 37:37-38, ESV)

It was a wonderful deed for the king to give Queen Esther Haman's wealth and to make Mordecai the second in command. But the law setting the day for all the Jews to be killed still stood.

The king's reaction to learning about Haman's action apparently came from being embarrassed and feeling manipulated by Haman. It doesn't appear that he was overly concerned about saving the Jews.

Queen Esther, who found the courage to expose Haman, now found the courage to ask the king to help reverse the effects of the law. She "fell at his feet and wept" (Es. 8:3) as she pleaded with him. She asked him to "avert the evil plan of Haman" (Es. 8:3).

The king extended the golden scepter to Esther after she fell at his feet and wept. No one except certain court officials could enter the king's presence or speak to him without permission. Earlier, when Esther approached the king without his consent, the king extended his golden scepter toward her (see Es. 5:2). This implied consent to be there. By doing it here, some Bible scholars think Esther risked her life again to plead on behalf of the Jews.

**2**  Every believer is to intercede (pray) for others. Read the following list. Beside each one, write the name of someone who needs your prayers. Take a moment to pray for each one. Feel free to add additional names with other needs.

1. Someone sick

2. An unbeliever

3. Someone with family issues

4. Someone needing a job

5. Others

Queen Esther appealed emotionally to the king. She asked him two questions: how could she "bear to see the calamity" (Es. 8:6) that was coming to the Jews? And how could she "bear to see the destruction" (Es. 8:6) of her race? In other words, she wanted the king to know that she couldn't emotionally handle what was about to happen.

The king reminded Esther and Mordecai that he ordered Haman's death on the gallows and gave Esther Haman's wealth. Then he agreed Mordecai was authorized to write whatever he wished, seal it with the signet ring, and publish it throughout the kingdom.

**3** Wisdom often is needed when dealing with sensitive issues. Why do you think Queen Esther allowed her emotions, both in what she did and what she said, to show to the king? Why do you think Mordecai remained silent while Esther was speaking?

_____

_____

_____

_____

_____

_____

_____

_____

_____

_____

Instead of telling Mordecai and Esther what to write, the king told them to write whatever they wished and issue it in his name. But the challenge wasn't as easy as it sounded. The new law or edict couldn't simply nullify the one issued two months earlier. The laws of the Medes and Persians could not be changed under any conditions.

As before, the king's scribes were ordered to come to the capital. These men had the responsibility of copying the law exactly as it was issued. They gathered on the twenty-third day of Sivan, the month on the Persian calendar that corresponds with May-June today. This would be exactly two months and ten days after Haman tricked the king into signing the Jewish death order.

The order was written for the satraps, the governors, and the officials in the kingdom. The author of the book of Esther noted again that the kingdom stretched from India to Ethiopia and included 127 provinces. Because this vast area included various languages, the law was written in all the languages of the kingdom.

Unlike the first decree ordering the death of the Jews, this law also was written in the language of the Jews. In fact, they were mentioned first. Government leaders, along with the common people, knew this meant that the Jews were elevated in the mind of the king.

As soon as the scribes finished, the copies of the law were given to special couriers riding special horses. Their sole purpose was to take the copies to the various regions as fast as possible.

The law written by Mordecai and issued in the king's name allowed the Jews to defend themselves against anyone who tried to kill them, including any government official or group. Every leader knew the message from the king was clear: they weren't to bother, harass, or kill any Jew.

**4** **Throughout the book of Esther, the faithfulness of God to His people is evident. What are some ways God has demonstrated His faithfulness to you in the past? What are some ways God is demonstrating His faithfulness to you every day? What are some ways you believe God will be faithful in the future?**

Mordecai, in his new role as second in command, went from the king's presence into the presence of the people. He was wearing his royal robes of blue and white, a golden cord, and a purple robe of fine linen. The people in the capital were excited when they saw him. Mordecai received the admiration and respect that Haman craved. People knew that Mordecai was a humble man of character who had the best interest of the citizens in mind.

The Jews "had light and gladness and joy and honor" (Es. 8:16). That is, they didn't have to hide their identities anymore. They could be happy and rejoice. Above all, the other races honored them as fellow citizens.

The joy experienced by the people, especially the Jews in Susa spread throughout the kingdom. In every city and province, there was rejoicing among the Jews. So much so that the Jews had a feast and a holiday. They had a reason to celebrate - they thought they were going to die, but now they were going to live.

Esther chapter eight concludes with an unusual statement. The writer wrote that many of the Gentiles, or non-Jewish people, declared themselves Jews. The Hebrew phrase translated "became Jews" (Es. 8:17) is found only here in the Old Testament. Bible scholars differ on its meaning. Some think many of the people began to follow the God of the Israelites by abandoning their worship of idols. Most, however, think the phrase means that the people took the side of the Jews and welcomed them into their society.

Chapter eight of the book of Esther opens with Queen Esther weeping on behalf of the Jews. It ends with everyone rejoicing. The queen's courage and love for her people saved their lives.

**5** How we respond to bad news often affects how we respond to good news. Read Esther 4:1-3 and 4:15-16. Then read Esther 8:16-17. When hearing bad news, how does brokenness and praying open the door for God to work? What do you think would have happened if the Jews grew angry and rebelled against God? How does earnestly praying for something allow us joy when it happens?

# Further Study

Believers are to intercede and pray for others. Read Genesis 18:20-33. What qualified Abraham to intercede for the people of Sodom? What do you think was Abraham's motive for interceding? Why do you think he was satisfied with God sparing the city for 10 righteous people? Read Genesis 19:23-29. Why did God destroy the city? What effect did Abraham's prayer have? What is the difference between the residents of Sodom and the Jews in the Book of Esther?

## Journal Your Journey

# Prayer Requests

# Week Eight

# 8

# Courage to Stand :
## COURAGE TO CELEBRATE

"Therefore the Jews of the villages, who live in the rural towns, hold the fourteenth day of the month of Adar as a day for gladness and feasting, as a holiday, and as a day on which they send gifts of food to one another."

Esther 9:19

---

Everybody loves a celebration! Whether it is community-wide or just an immediate family, celebrating a milestone is fun. The food, the laughter, and the excitement make celebrations special.

Most celebrations have one common trait: they are celebrating something worth celebrating. The Fourth of July, for example, is an American national celebration, celebrating freedom from the British. A birthday party celebrates someone's life, having lived another year. The celebration comes from remembering.

Most of the book of Esther is filled with suspense. Will the Jews die? Will Queen Esther find the courage to speak to the king? What will the king do? Will Haman succeed in his plan to kill Mordecai?

Once these questions are answered and the Jews are saved from death, it is time to celebrate. But first, they would have to defend themselves against those who hated the Jews and wanted to kill them.

**1** **What is your favorite annual celebration? Why do you enjoy celebrating it? What are you remembering?**

_____

_____

_____

_____

_____

_____

_____

_____

_____

Nine months passed from the decree Mordecai wrote until the appointed day of death from the law Haman wrote. It gave the Jews time to arm themselves and prepare to defend themselves.

It is important to note why those who hated the Jews couldn't kill them before that appointed day. It would have been illegal, but on the day set by Haman's law, the Jews could be murdered, and their possessions could be taken without any repercussions. However, Mordecai's decree allowed the Jews to kill those who would kill them without consequences on the same day. The Jews, too, could take the possessions of those they killed in defense without violating the law.

Before the day of conflict dawned, the installation of Mordecai as second in command changed the attitude of people toward the Jews. The author of the book of Esther noted that the reverse occurred. The non-Jewish population feared Mordecai in particular.

In the nine months before the day of conflict, all the government officials realized the power that Mordecai and the Jews held and the influence that he had on the king. As a result, the government officials sided with the Jews and helped them.

Since the original order required these government officials to kill all the Jews in their area, it would appear the Jews had nothing to fear. Like Haman, however, there were many in the kingdom that still hated the Jews. They would try to use the original law as an excuse to kill the Jewish people.

**Read the following Scriptures and note the way God worked by causing fear to come into the hearts of others.**

**Genesis 35:5**

**Deuteronomy 2:25**

**Joshua 2:11**

**II Chronicles 20:29**

**Acts 5:5**

The Jews took the initiative and destroyed their enemies. In the capital city of Susa, the Jews killed 500 men, including the ten sons of Haman. Their names are listed (see Es. 9:7-8), but they aren't mentioned anywhere else in the Bible.

They, like their father, probably hated the Jews. Angry about their father's death and their loss of power, they probably tried to turn as many people as possible against the Jews. They probably were among the first aggressors against the Jews that day.

When the king heard about the death of Haman's ten sons and the other 500 people, he asked Queen Esther if she had another wish and, if so, he would grant it. Esther asked if the Jews in Susa could have one more day to destroy their enemies. Furthermore, she wanted the ten sons of Haman to be hung on the gallows like their father. Although they were already dead, hanging Haman's sons on the gallows would be a public display of the wrong they did.

Today, during the Feast of Purim, when the reader in the synagogue reads the Book of Esther, he reads the names of Haman's ten sons in one breath because they all died together.

Esther's wish to extend the time in Susa for the Jews to defend themselves was granted by the king. The next day the Jews killed an additional 300 people. Queen Esther probably asked for the additional day because some may have attempted to kill the Jews but failed. She wanted to make sure everyone in Susa that hated the Jews died.

**3**      **Parents affect how their children view other people. Haman's hatred for Mordecai affected his sons. How can a parent's views of the following affect the thinking of their children?**

**Different race or nationality**

**Different economic status**

**Different political views**

In the other provinces, the Jews killed 75,000 people. They acted only on the day permitted in Mordecai's decree. Based on this number, there were approximately 600 people killed in each province.

Although the law permitted the Jews to take the possessions of those they killed, they didn't. Three times the author stated that the Jews "laid no hands on the plunder" (Es. 9:10, 9:15-16). From the beginning of the Jewish race, God did not allow the Jews to take anything from the enemies they destroyed. Instead, they were to destroy everything.

Following the allowed days for defending themselves, the Jews celebrated and feasted. Part of their celebration was giving food as gifts, a practice that would continue with the Feast of Purim. Giving food as a gift often symbolized God's plan and purpose for His people. For example, the Hebrew word translated "gifts of food" (Es. 9:19) is translated as "portion" in Psalm 16:5.

**4** Why do you think God never allowed the Israelites to keep the possessions of their enemies? Why do you feel God requires full commitment from us? What Bible verses or stories can you use to justify your opinion? Write your answer here.

**5**    **Mordecai, in his order for the Jews to celebrate this feast annually, carefully described what happened. Using Esther 9:22 as a guide, what transformation did Mordecai say that God did?**

He turned _____ into _____ and He turned
_____ into a _____ .

The Jews agreed with Mordecai's command. They annually remembered how Haman was the enemy of the Jews and used Mordecai's refusal to bow to him as an excuse to destroy the Jewish race in the Persian kingdom.

While Haman plotted his evil plan, God was working behind the scene. Haman cast lots to determine the day that the Jews should be killed. Miraculously, the lots indicated a day far into the future. It gave the Jews time to prepare. Now, the Jews would celebrate for all time how God turned the plan of Haman against him and his family.

The Jews called the celebration the Feast of Purim. Purim is the plural of "pur," the Babylonian word that is translated "lot." Both the singular, "pur," and the plural, "purim," are found only in the book of Esther.

Each year the Jews begin the celebration by fasting on the first day. They go to the synagogue where the book of Esther is read. Every time Haman is mentioned in the story, the people present respond by saying, "May he be accursed!"

The Jews return the second morning to the synagogue. The book of Esther, along with Moses' encounter with the Amalekites, is read. Following the service, the people go home and celebrate with food and gifts. The Jews send food to the poor so they can join the celebration.

The Torah written by Moses created five Jewish feasts. Each of these recalled how God established the nation of Israel. With the Feast of Purim, the Jews would celebrate how God protected their survival. Later, the Jews would add Hanukkah to remember their deliverance from Antiochus Epiphanies in the second century B.C.

**6** Remembering special events to give praise to God is a healthy spiritual exercise. Beside each of these events, write the date (if you know) that it occurred. If you don't know, select a day to celebrate it. Start putting the event on your yearly calendar and take time to praise the Lord on that day for His work in your life. In addition to this list, you may want to add others.

Day of salvation

Being baptized

Committing to a church

Started volunteering

Healed from sickness

Other events

The book of Esther concludes with Queen Esther writing a second decree to legally establish the festival, echoing what Mordecai had written earlier and with an emphasis on Mordecai's position in the kingdom. By doing so, Esther becomes the only woman in the Bible that established a religious practice still in use today.

The three verses of chapter ten illustrate how Mordecai worked to assure that the Jews were treated fairly and that peace was maintained between them and with them.

## Further Study

As believers, we have times we celebrate. We celebrate the birth of Christ at Christmas and His resurrection at Easter. But the New Testament calls us to celebrate what Christ has done for us every Sunday. Read Acts 2:42-47. How are believers supposed to celebrate every Sunday? Where are we to do it? Why should we do it? What effects should it have on our lives?

# Journal Your Journey

# Prayer Requests

# Additional Notes

# WOMEN OF JOY ™

## Are you ready for the best weekend ever?

When is the last time you had a weekend away to focus on your relationship with friends and, most importantly, God?

Women of Joy is a three day, two-night weekend where thousands of women gather in the name of Jesus to worship the Lord, study God's Word, and fellowship with friends.

**It is the original Women's Weekend Getaway. It is truly the best weekend ever!**

Meet our speakers and artists, and find the Women of Joy event nearest you at **womenofjoy.org.**